Rooms Overhead

Also by Betsy Sholl

Changing Faces
Appalachian Winter

ROOMS OVERHEAD

Betsy Sholl

Alice James Books
Cambridge, Massachusetts

Copyright © 1986 by Betsy Sholl

The publication of this book was made possible with support from the National Endowment for the Arts, Washington, D.C., and from the Massachusetts Council on the Arts and Humanities, a state agency whose funds are recommended by the Governor and appropriated by the State Legislature.

Library of Congress Catalogue Card Number 86-70727
ISBN 0-914086-66-9 (hardbound)
ISBN 0-914086-67-7 (paperback)

Designed by George Benington
Composed by Portland Litho
Paste-up by Claire Putnam
Cover Illustration by Karen J. Wellenkamp

Grateful acknowledgement is made for the use of lines from Sappho translated by Mary Barnard in *Sappho, A New Translation*, by Mary Barnard, University of California Press, Berkeley, California, 1962.

Grateful acknowledgement is also made to the editors of the following publications in which versions of some of these poems first appeared: *The Agni Review, The Beloit Poetry Journal, Field, The Greenfield Review, Journal of Kentucky Studies, Poetry Northwest, Radix, Second Growth, Sojourners, The Virginia Quarterly Review, West Branch.*

"The Flood" is anthologized in *Poems of the Third Epoch*, Carmarthen Oak Press, 1980, and is included in *Common Ground*, an anthology of Appalachian poetry.

A grant from *Appalachian Woman Grants for Writers* enabled some of these poems to be written.

Printed in The United States of America

Alice James Books are published by the Alice James Poetry Cooperative, Inc.

Alice James Books
138 Mount Auburn Street, Cambridge, Massachusetts 02138

For Doug, Matthew and Hannah

Contents

III

I

Elegy

Last night ashen as a runner
the old woman burst the ribbon
stretched across her bed
and finished the race.
I'll catch up later.
Tell them to go ahead,

those men with red lights
revolving on their cars
snatching the grief from my hands,
leaving what? Silence,
nervous air, dregs.

Is it true
nothing vanishes in nature?
The undertaker
breaks the old woman's jaw
to hide the last gasp
that freed her.

The terrible weight
at my shoulders tells me
I was meant to fly.

Tell them I'm not coming
in their black procession
moving solemn as insects
perfectly structured, grief
parceled out, each
weeping an equal share.

If there were time
before the deluge begins
I would read through old junk,
summertime letters from young men
whose names I barely recognize
on the fundraising list
my college sends to make me ashamed.

I'm ashamed enough already
finding in the same box
in my grandmother's frail script
her last words to me: Life is real,
life is earnest, and the grave
is not its goal.

Tell those men waiting
beneath the building
they won't need their nets after all.
I will weep.

I will splash out this sorrow.
I know I can fly. But first
I will come down the stairs
and shake the flesh of their hands
earnestly, one by one.

Whitecaps

The bay is cold, heavy under a north wind.
Whitecaps keep coming. Little sheep,
the wind prods them along.
Waves of refugees, old people rocking.
My grandmother, her vision lost
in the hold of a ship, fingers
too numb to knit, though they never stop moving.

Is she a message the wind wants sent?
It brings tears to my eyes.
It cuts through my coat
till I'm naked as she was, hairless
between my legs.

I see her getting stripped:
Where were you born?
Her breasts sag like wet clothes on the line.
Can you read? Can you cook, sew?
No lice, literate. They pass her through.
Wind lulls, gusts. Cold and strong October.

Incredible sky. Piles of fleece.
She says, *Come, let's walk.*
Wind pulls at our voices, little kinks
of yarn the gulls snatch. She's 14,
about to board her first train.
Her father's hands cup her face and press
as if he could stop the noise, the steam,
the huge wheels beginning to roll.

We go past scrub oak, pine, black roads
studded with white pebbles and shells, cattails,
the wild steppes of the bay. From that train
she watches mountains drop into the sea.
Her sister moans in fever. A man puts his hand
on her breast and, though she stares straight ahead,
she does not try to move it.

Now alone, wind in my coat, I feel hands
fitting a sweater across my nipples
plucking each one between finger and thumb.
You're growing up, my lamb.

Should I tell her there's blood on my legs,
smell of seaweed at low tide, smell of her
when she's worried. Am I going to die?

Oh yes, she says, *again and again*
handing me these threads, knots to untie.

Edges

It isn't myself I watch
leaning out over the bridge,
heart racing jump! jump!
It's those fins, swift as thought
gliding through feathery weeds.

Tiny bubbles rise to the surface
and snap. I can't see where
they come from. My own eyes
on the water block the view.

Echo, astonish me.
Say something I haven't heard.

I want the world without screens,
the edge without rails,
to be free of these lenses, this skin.

A fish nudges my reflection,
leaps right through my eye.
I ripple and blur.

It's true. We are what we see.
I am sunlight, silvery scales
breaking through shadow,
circles expanding. Echo,

nothing you say can stop me.
I'm going to love the whole world,
to jump.

Releasing Grandfather

The old man's full of accusations —
what's under my dress? what's on my breath?
have I become a woman? He thinks I have
boys hidden under my bed.

He goes off on a bus without speaking,
heads someplace not on the map
like the farm where he was born once,
and now worries once isn't enough.

Two weeks he's gone, no explanation.
Comes back, stares through my window.
I'm changing my clothes.
He shakes a bony finger.

All flesh is grass, he says, jabbing his cane.
I push the mower, watch clumps of grass
fly out from the sides, insects
jump from the path like sparks.

*

Oh, that hatchet face,
that twig of a finger poked at my eye.
Years later I still pull the shade.
Then tonight it snaps.

I bolt up in bed,
look out the window, see
lamplight on gold frames, hollow
cheek, eye. Good Lord, it's me —

black branches spread over my face —
how did I get so stern, so thin?
A truck passes and the field flares up.
I remember before he said it was wrong

to open my arms and spin among the cedars'
dark fragrant limbs — I turned faster and faster
till the whole woods tilted and grass rose
like skirts swirling at my legs.

Album

for my father

I picked up shells from the waves,
lifted photographs wet and dripping
from the darkness:

Flare of wave against a loose plank,
footprints on dunes —

I looked in water,
in the stiffened swirls of wood

This is the pier that was built
by jutting out firmly
to soften the waves

They go on and on
Nobody stops them
You never finished the roll

I posed for years trying to smile
to make you appear in the foam
at the end of that jetty

Now on the faces of children
turning in the light
I catch a second of your grin

Then they're off
racing across the dunes
leaping the line of spring rubble

A wave peaks, sharp as a paper's edge
They dive, just as it crumples

The Stutterer

Under the pillow at night
I whisper stories dramatic and feathery —
all *w*'s and *f*'s, *s*'s and hard, hard *g*'s.

In the morning my mouth sticks together.
I can't even spit.

Everyone grabs my words.
They guess what I mean,
even when I switch midsentence,
sounds twisting themselves into lies.

One side of my brain is glass.
The other is hammers.

I do try to relax.
I take deep breaths, start slowly
pulling the tangle of worms.

It rouses, begins to rattle, to hiss.
Steam, steam. No vent.
Everyone watches, ready to scatter.

Inside my head sentences build
stone tablets. I throw them down,
all those rules broken across the ground.

But who can be silent?
Someone asks; I give directions.

People think I've seen something shocking
like the jagged steps to heaven,
time's curved and faceted reflector glass.

That's why my words won't start,
why tongues are quick as matches
to snatch what I say.

Fire! fire! fire!

The touch of that finger engraves a stone.
The flames leap in my throat.
Wind sock, fish net, splintering star —

Milkweed

I love wind   I love fire
When it puts on long sleeves
And leaps at the grate
Red scarves slacken and snap

That's the life
Milk sings into the pail
The pond's full of stars
Pumpkins in the field break their gags

I love sparks
Tossed across the floor
Shiny as water
Before it soaks up the grime

But Old Woman, what's the use?
I'm limp hair, pajamas
Elbows and knees
Sticking out like broom handles
Breath sour as the sponge
Left in the scrub bucket

"Fetch this, fetch that" —
Those two horseheads, my sisters

I want to be beautiful
What must I do?

She gives me a new dress
She gives me till midnight
She has a stick in her hand
She knows how to use it

It figures, half a wish
A ride one way, one shoe

But walking home in the moonlight —
White wisps of clouds
Tree shadows lacing the road
Dried cornstalks blowing like streamers

I kick off my crinolines and dance
Long after twelve, waltz into the garden
Skirts loose and flaring
Godmother laughing   Tufts of milkweed
Flung from the stick in her hand

The Lives of Birds

My mother
at her bedroom window
binoculars and bird book —

I'd stumble into her room
rubbing my eyes. She'd say, "Birds.
It's early. Go back to sleep."

For years they made her weep,
disappearing in leaves, untouchable
pheasants and buntings, finches, doves.

What would she think of
magnifying those brief flashes
across the yard —
my father's hand resting in hers?

Once, I climbed into her bed
while she was sleeping. "Jack,"
she murmured, putting her legs through mine.

She joined the volunteer first aid.
My sisters and I heard whippoorwills
in the night when sirens went off.

We heard her car move down the road.
Then the birds started talking —
"They die. They never come back."

5 o'clock, she'd get home,
find us in her bed
and take the chair by the window.

She'd been driving with sirens.
She'd been mouth on mouth with a stranger.
How quiet it must have seemed —

a few doves in the cedar, a cardinal,
a jay. She'd take up the binoculars,
focus the lens.

The Goose-Girl

1

I toss a stone
and the face scatters.
But it comes right back.

As a child I wanted to be
invisible, to see light
rushing through water.

I watched geese grumble and hiss,
saw them pull at weeds
as if trying to unplug the pond.

What's real? I'd ask my sisters.
Right here, where I'm standing
is something else standing as well?

Silly goose, they laughed.
But I couldn't stop asking:
what color? what animal
would you be? what do you think
when you hear the word mother?
What frightens you most?

2

Now the water's like my child
repeating what I say.

You're too close to the edge.
You're too close to the edge.

Did you hear me?
Did you hear me?

I mean it.
I mean it.

Walking around the pond
phrase after phrase —
tired of hearing myself
I lean over the edge.

I want to put my hands
on those shoulders,
bring the child so close
I jump into her eyes.

They get bigger and bigger,
circles, striations of blue.
I'm upside down, gliding
through loose tangles,
undulant vines.

O, I come up exhaling
one long breath of surprise.

3

Rain stitches down the pond,
swan feathers, goose
down, wings of maples
too heavy to fly.

I pick my way
through the gray slip of dung.
What do you want? I ask the face
on the water. *Golden egg or real?*

I want the real, the sound of it cracking,
shiny yolk spilling like the birth of the sun.
And when that's done, I want to be free of wanting.

The geese sit plumped on the lawn, soggy pillows.
It's hard to believe they've got wings,
voices that pierce the sky.

Remember that, I tell the face on the water,
the child dawdling behind, the old woman ahead
in shoes too big for herself.

Remember how wind gets hold of them,
and they stretch out their necks
as though called to this,
as though nothing else mattered
they hurl themselves into the sky.

Three Graveyards

1

My mother's grandmother brought three children
from England. One died on ship, one here
of fever. The baby withered inexplicably,
a plant shocked to its thinnest roots.
She had five more.

Still, my mother remembers
her grandmother in an apron
riding the trolley to the public cemetery,
grief having pierced her as she bent
in the garden clipping parsley or roses.

Once on a small stone
my mother found her own name.
Light as you'd touch lips, her fingers
traced it, exactly the same.
Then, dizzy, she touched *May* and *November*
just one year before she was born.

Riding home in the open car,
scent of roses on her grandmother's hands,
tracks gleaming with late sun,
she flushed and shivered, whispering
Beatrice? Beatrice?

2

Our daughter smells milk
and nuzzles at the buttons of my shirt.
A hundred years ago she'd be dead
of her infection.

Our son straddles a stone
pretending to gallop.
It's all right. Let him shout.

I am the daughter of widows.
Many times in stony gardens
I have stood back watching
my mother, my grandmother,
faces of glass.

I have seen cracks
where old women's flesh
was shattered and glued.

My mother's eyes gleamed like crystal.
If I spoke too loudly, if I bumped her —
would she spill?

3

Do you remember when we lay thigh to thigh
in the cemetery, running shoots of grass
across each other's lips? Wind blew the edges
of papers sticking out from our unopened books.
Inside our clothes we were rivers rising.
The lightest breeze spilled us over.
We were both so young. You'd never seen
anyone grieve. I didn't know my body
could fill up and swell, creatures
churning inside me. That whole afternoon
surrounded by stones, we saw nothing
but light blowing strands of hair
across our faces.

Riding Hood

My daughter makes songs from the words
she hears, mixing *august barley grief*
into a broth sloshing inside its jar.

There's no wolf in her skipping
red-shirted song.
Where did I learn to fear?

Surely I am happy
hearing her beside me
singing as I used to sing
in the back seat of the car
serenading the black trees
at the edge of the road
as the bald astonished moon
flew out of the branches.

We walk down the street gathering leaves.
What stirs the trees? One of my mother's
long sighs, one of her words meaning *loss,*
that squint in her eyes looking at all
that might gobble us up.

But, Mother, I wasn't eaten.
Poor though we were, the dog didn't snarl.
Grandmother lived next door.
I never entered a stranger's car.

For all your worry,
don't you think you were a fine woman
for me to study, to learn by heart?

August august barley grief
and blessings flow. My daughter sings
on and on. *My mommy my mommy*
my mom-mee-mom. Why should I grieve?

We sit on the steps humming.
The moon rises through the trees, lips pursed
in the first quizzical *O* of a song.
So what if death cruises the block
in his shiny car leaning out the window
calling to her — My daughter
shake your yellow hair at him.

II

Farmwife

The woman who has nodded to me from her porch
for weeks, still nods now, bobs her head
leading me inside to see
21 grandchildren posed on a shelf,
sills full of colored glass.

Twice, I heard, she left her husband
and then returned.

He stays outside with the dogs,
hollering them away from the barn.

Chickens flutter and squall,
leaving patches of brown feathers.

She says she's been nodding 26 years.
The doctor calls it "the trembles,"
but she knows something sharper
is pecking her brain.

Twice his fists have hit,
knocked her against the wall.
Twice she's returned

to faces of grandchildren
perfectly still in the tilt
of their frames, glass
shining on every sill,

to hens squawking themselves into trees
whenever a dog comes near:

She sweeps up the puddles
of brown and white feathers
that fear sends flying,

pours them into ticking
to cushion her relentless,
affirming head.

Job's Wife

Then his wife said to him, "Do you still
hold fast your integrity?
Curse God and die."   Job 2:9

Yes, I said it.
And I told him to pull out his hair,
scream till his eyes turned black.

Some integrity,
scraping himself with broken pots.
An expert on God.
I'm an expert on mustard plaster,
bad breath.

On ten children —
their shoulders, their eyes,
the curve of their buttocks
I knew better than my own hands.

So you're God.
Tell me I'm straw, chaff, mist.

Tell me the sea has springs
deep and cold as dreams
that make me wake exhausted.

Enough thunder.
What have you done
with my children?

*

Not one runner makes dust
coming toward me, undoing the curse.
I cry till I'm spit inside out
but fire doesn't reverse.
Wind won't swallow itself.

[37]

Look at these hands. Ten stiff
children dug into my palms.
I make them straighten and bend.
I sift through ashes
and smear my face.

Standing at the river, I see how
only my shadow is unmoved on the water.
It's an absence that takes my shape.
I too am swirling.

                    *

I watch women spin. Flax
goes into their wheels, stiff
and broken. Soft strands come out
as if God were weaving new cloth
from the stricken fields.

As if I could stretch out my hands
and God would restore ten new children.

Though wind rise, tent collapse
and bury them all again,
I would not refuse.

I would not refuse them
starlight in the well, mist
quiet as hair on their faces.
I cannot deny wind swelling, leaves
turning white, across the field
thunder breaking its gate,
the door swung open.

Wisps

for S—

She sits in the window looking at webs,
a room full of jewels.
If she could slip through those strands
without breaking the shiny beads —

on the other side
silk would spin from her mouth,
if she said *wing,* she'd fly.
If she said *father,* the door would open.

    He'd walk in, move his fingers
    through her hair, down her back.

Now her mother calls
but she doesn't understand
supper, hurry, wash.

She chalks on a board, lines weaving
round and round till a pattern takes hold,
tiny face in a maze —

    and he is there again
    rubbing between her legs,
    crooning hush, hush
    though she hasn't said a word.

At night she runs
till the sheet holds her in knots.
Her hair is so tangled one morning
her mother cuts it.

She remembers the wisps falling
down her neck, her back,
that fine net of shivers
dropping over her body.

[39]

Through the Looking Glass

"But 'glory' doesn't mean a 'Nice knock-down
argument,' " Alice objected.

I sit in a room filled with plaques
honoring my stepfather, certificates
framed with glass and thin wood.
His legs are thin. His temper is glass.
He is very famous along these walls.

When the sun comes in the window
the gold seals beam at it
showing off their fine embossing.

O O O how sad the glass is.
It wants to be a real window.

My stepfather enters the room.
He wants something too. It keeps moving
one shelf above wherever he looks.
It slips through the ceiling.

I remember a boat.
I can't hear what he says, we're moving so fast.
I love wind in my hair. I squeeze his hand
and he puffs out his cheeks, makes his eyes bulge
till I have to laugh.

Then we're back to these walls.
He wants to give me advice: Money
and words. "There's glory for you."
We both sigh.

I mean: Notice me. I want to touch you.

He clears his throat: "We've had enough
of this. Now I want to know what you're doing
with the rest of your life."

Strong wind rattles the plaques.
All that ink, those curly letters —
when the sun shines you can't read a word.

Whatever Moves

I may be saved yet.
My grandmother's praying.
She's saying to anyone who'll listen:
Throw out the curtains. Stop
washing so much. God has no sex.

Don't cut the grass! she calls
after young men with sickles.
Wind nests there. Here it comes.

Then she's gone,
this old woman of mine, drifting off
in her chair on the boardwalk.

Water and sky turn pink
as the shawl on her legs.
A smile like foam flickers
then slips through sand.

She's gone off ahead
someplace people forget to write from,
someplace that shocks their bodies,
the roots of their minds.

Grass, trees, curtains,
the loose board on the stairs —
whatever moved she followed.

Tired of church, she said,
angel fossils in old walls.

Over there, she pointed, and I saw
everything solid ripple,
invisible flames converting
water and sand into light.

[42]

Tonight I Am Mending Clothes

I use old cloth on the knees, stitch boldly.
The dress I hem more carefully,
camouflaging the thread, an animal in grass.

I think of Dorcas, raised from the dead,
stitching long hours in weakening light.
Her name means gazelle. In Hebrew, Tabitha.
She is called a disciple full of good works.

I picture her in a window at dusk, shoulders
gathered around the needle's sharp persistence.
Rain falling. Sparrows in mulberry trees.

Hands basting in and out, lips moving —
Christ, have mercy — she looks up
and a sudden jolt rends her coarse fabric
into a garment of light.

Sound travels more slowly.
Feeling the frayed edges where she had been
torn from them, the mourners weep.

From my distance, I'd like to know
what of her was left to hear, "Tabitha, arise"?
And did those words wash over like waves
moving her to shore, or did she have to choose,

to fight the current and strain to return?
I feel pins and needles inside,
something quicker than blood threading my veins.

When she stands, everything the mourners hold
as fixed and true bursts at the seams.
News runs through the city of Joppa.
God mended her. Not one stitch shows.

[43]

Loving Mammon

I saw you in the paper, with a shovel
breaking ground for the new bank.
Your mouth was full of teeth.

Now on the front page
you're getting the keys. You smile,
but your eyes are blank. I'm afraid
death has already begun
to steal you away from your money.

I've seen you at corners
jingling the change in your pockets,
eyeing the old men who doze,
their clothes thick with newspaper,
the trials of the world.

Is it true
our possessions are computed against us,
cards in hand at the end of the game,
weights tied to our feet?

Oh, the river is deep.
At low tide you can hear those who've sunk,
endlessly counting, endlessly missing a stone.

Maples in Pittsburgh

This yellow tree
black branches full of applause —
Martha, skirts flying, long ribbons
in our hair, that word Mother sniffed at,
frivolous.

A thousand hands beckon.
We step out your back door, look up
and we're leaves in the wind, skirts
suddenly lifted.

A clear day downtown,
crowds swirl, elbows and thighs.
Martha, is heaven so perfect
we won't get bored?

We're going two at a time
up the church steps, returning the music
you've practiced till you can play
the way I see the color of leaves
when I close my eyes.

Inside the huge dark
our voices stop, our pace slows
as if stilled by a spirit whose musing
is stronger than us both.

Hushed, scowled at for squirming
on the stiff pews, we didn't know back then
that above the ceiling's two thousand
plaster curls is one continuous
ebb and flow, an invisible extravagance
the trees embody and release.

Outside leaves flare like candles
the wind ignites, like divine sparks
smoldering on sidewalks and fences,
on cars, wherever they fall.

I pull the pins from my hair, pull you
down the steps into this shining ovation.

Learning to Love the Sky

for Margaret

It isn't easy to believe
the sky comes down to the ground
here, not just in the distance
behind the corner store where darkness
bleeds at the edges, but here, to say —
it is sky I'm breathing, as if that
implied heaven as well and perhaps
required something of us, like the effort
my daughter makes with her blue crayon
filling in between flowers, fence posts,
the branches of trees.

Through first tentative maple leaves
I watch young men gathered at the corner,
hunching their backs to the rain.
It's easy to see they aren't watching
the sky, not with their necks craned
till they feel dwarfed and dizzy
and glad enough to spin as my daughter
often does walking home from the store
tossing the bread.

I walk myself now through this sodden group
to avoid the sewer backed up in the street.
Curses fall steady and impersonal as rain.
Fifteen, twenty young men aimlessly spar,
pass joints. I touch one's shoulder,
take his face in my hands, and peer
into his eyes as if the sky wrapped us
in one blanket we could share to keep warm.
At least I imagine this

as my gaze lifts above the storefronts
in currents beyond my senses where the huge
maples tremble. How frail they make us seem.
I hear voices, fricatives falling like seeds
on concrete. I see a fist shoot out
toward the sky then lower its aim. Two men
roll on the ground. One gets up.

That's all I know. What I saw.
And the thick sky loosening, sunset glowing
in puddles at our feet, as if the ground
could roll over and open its eyes.

Skiing on Water

for R.J.K.

One year I took the wrapping off a carton of powdered milk
and with the silver inside made a moon, a path across water
shining between two dark hills. "Happy Birthday," I wrote.
You were 72. You answered, "Remembrance is the sweetest
flower — the older you grow the truer this seems."
What's left up ahead you called imponderable. *Heavy,*
I first thought, like footsteps moving toward a hill
that darkens as you approach.

Now, watching birds enter and reenter trees, beaks full
of string, twigs, bright strips of plastic from last year's
gardens, I remember that card, and how I had so little
money then. Yet so much was free — flowers every day
along the road, just growing wild. And there were
cardinals, orioles, indigo buntings in that yard.

These are starlings, little sparks blown through space,
blackening as they drop. But I've seen *skylings* as well,
drab as poverty in the shade, then flushed out — so rich
and blue you'd swear Plato was right, there's an essence
of sky, sea, blood unbroken, a world of light: a kingdom
where the poor rejoice without measure or cost, where scraps,
loose ends, our wrongs are converted like pieces of kite,
seeds passed through the dark digestion of birds
then dropped ready to sprout.

I first noticed light that afternoon at the river
when I was the only child you couldn't get up on skis.
I stared till I saw coins spinning on the water
as if the sun were making wishes for me, and you
were right — all I had to do was trust, lean back,
bend my knees a little.

[49]

I'd been trying so long the sky was that late afternoon
luminous blue you can't find in paint or cloth or anyone's
eyes, the kind of gift that comes when you get fed up
and look another way. I can still see you half turned
in the boat, waiting for my signal. But the skis
were crossed, I had leaned back too far. I raised my hand
to say, "Go on without me," and the rope tightened.
I pulled back to stop you and was up, stooped over,
knock-kneed, skimming the water on long strange feet.

You said I'd never forget this, and it's true.
In the hardest times I think — what can I let go of or yank
to surprise myself? I think of you, weighed down by darkness,
and envision a shaft of light, a sudden turn of thought,
that moment you can step through and be caught up
faster than ever in wilder, more astonishing blue.

III

The Flood

Big Stone Gap, Virginia, 1977

Hiding from dust,
records of our lives
lie face down under the bed.
Certificates, diplomas, photographs,
love letters from a time
your thighs were so finely tuned
they rippled when my breath passed over.

Yet we never left our bodies.
Our flesh stayed in its banks.
We never expected to wake one morning
sheets thrown off the bed,
water swirling among trees,
water on the front step
slipping under our feet.

*

The river breaks through the house.
A trumpet. Our documents are raised.
They are all found lacking.
They cling to the walls, ink
running down in streaks.

*

Tonight, everything lost,
wanting rises, bursts
into fullness. Don't move, Love.
Let nothing divide us.
Don't even speak my name.

Tonight
because we let go
everything returns
with wings, a sprig in its mouth
then leaves.

*

We come back with rakes, gloves
and shots against typhoid.

The river makes small confused rills
around an oil tank, a sofa
it doesn't remember taking,
and we have to forgive.

We can't remember ourselves
the price of our mattress,
how much insurance we had
in that carton under the bed.

We throw out, we burn
photographs of my dead father,
his face bloated, covered with silt.

Silt rises through floorboards
each time we scrub. Smoke drifts
through blossoming trees.

My love
this flesh is rising.
It is level with your eyes.
It pours through my fingers.
It cannot be filed away.

[54]

Rooms Overhead

Thunder crashes like furniture dropped overhead,
those childhood angels rearranging their rooms.
Bureau, bookshelf, bed — grounded again, my daughter
shoves them across the floor, anger pumping her veins.
Soon I hear singing and know she is pleased
to be solving in space the problem that eluded her:
grownups refusing to be moved.

When I was a child and angels argued slamming doors,
I lolled, feet up the couch, head on the floor
envisioning other rooms silent and spare as ceilings
where weight couldn't go, nothing that breaks.
I couldn't budge a thing in the world outside
so I kept rearranging mine, loved waking to new
angles of light, books against a different wall
as if the same words might have powers I never guessed.

I heard all the shifting above, as if God wore boots
and strode through rooms kicking pianos, ripping drapes
while downstairs china rattled in the cabinet,
window cords broke. My father was already dead.
Now my grandfather began to mutter and glare,
my sister left on a boat for Africa.

Watching cracks in the ceiling I half expected it
to open on another world where the lost would be found:
a shaft of light, angels crowding my room, opening
drawers, spilling perfume. I stopped wanting those wings
and thought of a new language — shells, stones, hard things
you could line up and count, put in boxes, new words
strong as a shoe pounding the table.

Everyone looked up astonished as if the furniture had drained
from the room when my feathery whispers turned leather.
My mother wrote my sister, she didn't know what to do,
and my sister sent back letters to me, pictures of herself
surrounded by thatched roofs and vines. She sent words,
flashy ones that sounded like what they named: grasshopper,
thunder, a small rodent we don't even have in America.

All this was to say how big the world is, and don't be afraid.
She had a language full of phrases about how the sky could
blacken and crack like anger, the rain could pour,
and then miraculously be over, all forgiven, everything
clear, no sign except leaves dripping under a faultless
blue tropical sky.

Catechism

I begin as tradition advises
with a question for the rabbi.
How can the soul be free of its body?

But God knows they haven't ordained women long.
Her eyes are still bright. She leans forward,
peers into mine. Why would you want to?

Because it's there to be climbed.
Because I'm nearly forty and it's getting harder
to stay thin, wake rested, not weep in the afternoon.
It says *shame,* and *eat.* It's an imbecile
rocking itself at 5 in the morning
as if wind had no sway, trees turning above us
in March air so wild you know the invisible exists.

She leans back. I can't tell if she smiles
or frowns. What makes you want to see the invisible?
How would you know wind without flesh, hair?

I would be wind, I say.
But now this rabbi in woman form looks hard at me:
Then wind would change into fire.
You torture yourself.

But the body slumps and whines.
It's a dog, I say.

Her ears prick up. I know what she's thinking.
So feed it, she smiles. Let it keep you warm.
At night when its legs twitch, when a sound
breaks from its throat and wakes you,
listen.

The Root Canal

Leaning over my mouth he asks what I know
about Catherine of Russia and how she died.
I picture her reclined like this,
the horse above stampeding the air,
pulleys strained, some terrible need
rearing inside her.

He probes. I jump.
He pushes the needle
into my abscessed gum while I stare
at the light waiting to grow numb.

When he tips back the chair
I think of those narrow boats used
on distant islands to send off the dead.
I grip the sides, remember Saint Peter
stepping through waves the wind crumples
at his feet. He looks down, yells Save me!

No matter what he did
he couldn't spend that body.
They say where even his shadow fell
people were healed. Outside the temple
he takes a cripple by the hand and the man
doesn't walk, he leaps through the gate.

They say they had to turn him upside down
and hammer and shake
before his soul would come out,
before he'd leave us behind
in this narrow boat, foam flying,
wind rousing every hair on our bodies.

Barnegat Light

I like to come here
because everything dissolves.
My footprints, my glasses
my words — yes, those most of all.

My mother dissolves,
her look of distress
at the bad language I use
which is not even close
to what I hold in my head.

Here, the waves don't skip a beat.
I spit out names like stones
because I'm tired of pleasing,
speaking correctly
to keep things appearing.

I pick up pieces of shell.
Broken is such a crude word
for how old purposes evolve,
for climbing the steep circular staircase
around which inaudible whitecaps

form and dissolve like the motion
of somebody's lips calling in the distance.
All I can hear is the air peak and spill
from my lungs. Is it because I'm breathless
that my eyes are so clear? because the light

I see blowing across all that I see
erases me, and that invisible being
I know is moving, moves with me?

Matins

Powell Valley, Virginia

Every morning before we light the stove,
before we open the door and set out bones
on a plate for the wind to gnaw —
the day hangs white and shapeless in fog,
loose as the moon's frail gravity.

The cows, patient and faithful,
have not yet come out pacing foot by foot
mumbling their rosaries.
The mountains have not yet returned.
No fence posts, no stubble, no cars rusting.

Every morning the same:
we wake up brooding on chaos.
We shiver down to our knees
calling for cows, asking for trees,
for one streak of cloud pink as a rooster's comb
to stretch across the ridge.

We send our voices out
through the thick breath at our windows
and wait for an answer, a creak at the gate,
a dog to bark and set off a chain of hens rattling
across the field, with us repeating after it —
Today, today, by the ground we walk on,
we'll be patient and faithful.

Hallows

My children wake
rubbing their soft faces
wanting nothing with sugar for breakfast.

Their costumes lie in a heap,
all meanness gone out of them.
Wolf mask hangs on a chair upside down,
fright burst into laughter.

Pieces of plastic, brown bags,
scraps of old cloth
are scattered across the field.
All night leaves have fallen.

Now sun pours through bare limbs,
through window smudges
slanting across the floor. It
gleams on walls, the toaster,
the surface of coffee —

Saint Gratitude, Saint Joy
have arrived. Outside there follows
a long retinue of light.

Hanging Out the Wash

for my grandmother

Once you were real as the red blouse
wind flares in my hands.

I banged on your sheets.
Who's there, you called,
Little Gusto?

You didn't care what blew.
Rags, corsets, hernia belts
all flew from your lines.

Spittle flew when you laughed,
soap when you washed.
You threw loose hair to the birds.
Nothing was left to rot.

You called me *Sunshine,*
sang *Don't take it away.*
But the last time I kissed you
you stared straight ahead
and didn't kiss back.

Now wind flaps the sheets.
My daughter barges through.
She waves a dried pod
and white suds fill the air.

Wind lulls, then rises. It's you.
You've come for one last gust,
to smell sheets, to lift them,
inhabit sleeves once more.

What is it you want me to see?

[62]

Breathing Shallow

Midway through my life I wake up
and it's so clear and cold the trees
bristle up the backs of the mountains.

Light shines through the frozen wood
like wind through a threadbare coat.
I put it on, pull it close.

Everywhere the distance opens.
A flock of starlings rises up
like the ground itself throwing off gravity.

But first I must pass through this valley,
these trees thickening around me,
this forest so deep

I am tempted to stop, to lie down
surrounded by the howl of creatures
that seem to come from my own heart.

My eyes flicker. The paths disappear.
Only hunger can move me now, last feeling
that never sleeps, never forgets

this is the forest where people wander
in circles tightening slowly, the wood
they call dark, those who tell of the journey,

who take us so far, then stop midsentence
as though there, just through those briers,
is an open field of stars.

The Sting of Snow

I watch snow slide off branches
and embrace the plunge. Red wings flash
through the elms so quickly my eyes delay
the motion, stretch it out like a scarf
I catch and hold.

In Florida, at my mother's, the red birds
sing all night, hidden by branches of gardenia
whose fragrance completes her waking.
She drifts through the dark house
stirred by a longing that passes through air
like scent subtle enough to slip under stone.

I played in stinging ecstasies of snow
until my limbs were numb, believing
a deeper feeling would come if I just waited.
If I stared hard enough I knew I could make out
of the distance my father, alive, returning
in a circle of light that shimmered at the edges.

How I cried for giving in. Not for the sting in my hands
while my mother knelt tugging the frozen zipper, but for
something harder, for having hands at all, so clumsy
and brittle. Snow slid from the top of the Japanese elm.
Something red flashed in the water at the corner of my eye,
and I had no words, holding my frozen hands to her lips,
to tell her. Whatever I touched I wanted the ripple
along its edges, what wasn't there to appear.

My night is scentless and cold. I wake dreaming that the sky
has lain itself down near dawn on the steps of my house.
I go out, scoop up and taste what I once said in midsummer
was not a thing to be grasped. What did I know back then,
the insects flickering their effervescence like little stars
I plucked and set on my fingers, wanting to be picked by them
and drawn through darkness into air?

Tonight my mother touches the sharp edge of a table,
the satiny back of a chair, and as she walks
fragrance fills the room, scent of a harder
and more real presence beyond loss.

Forsythia

Again we come to these rains,
streets of dirty snow. The basket spills
as I step from the car into mud
across from the laundromat.
Adult Books. Violators will be towed.

The children bicker and whine.
I am not. You are too.
They pick towels from the slush
then dip them back in.

Once, forsythia lighted our way
down side streets of rain
through a hedge
to the chancellor's garden.

I remember walking to school —
those long rains, hedges
swollen, starting
to blister, the ache
of wood opening.

Rain ran down my shoulders,
soaked through my shirt.
My nipples were hard.
Wet bark from the trees
came off on my hands.

I touched ribs, hips, thighs,
water bursting from rock.

And next door that old woman,
stiff and pale behind lace,
scolding, scolding
as I cut through her blaze.

Cold water on my face
runs down my elbows and neck.
Eyes shut, pressed into a towel,
all I see is forsythia.

Spring Fragments

Like a hyacinth in
the mountains, trampled
by shepherds until
only a purple stain
remains on the ground
        Sappho,
            translated by Mary Barnard

1

There is a look some girls have,
freckled and hard, suspicious of women.
Now in front of the library
it's flashed on me.

Sappho, everything changes.
The wood blouses into petals
like a shy girl beginning to speak.
Now I too have children.

Almost blinded by the shimmering
of uncut grass at sunset, we talk
in clusters on the library steps
watching our daughters
drift down the street
toward the hurts that mellow.

I translate from longings:
dogwood, japonica, the soft
electricities of forsythia —
Forsythia, the name of the girl
I would have chosen to be.

2

On a narrow road crossing the mountain
I enter a lavender wood.
Everywhere, stretching around me
purple buds gleam on dark wet trees —
the strange dreams of my grandmother
dozing on the couch at noon
coming to a place of absolute transformation.

It is too beautiful.
I need a new body.

Two girls push each other, laughing
into a ditch. They run wet-footed
then stop to whisper, absently pulling off
whole branches of flowers.

Green tears fall from the elms.
I stand in the wind holding them.

3

Dogwood blossoms, lovely and full —
how endangered they are. The forsythia shines
as if laughing to think it could ever fall
into the matronly hedge of summer.
The japonica's last buds just opened
this morning and already they tremble.

Apple and plum alone embrace every change
as if they had mothers who prepared them well,
from a gnarled wisdom teaching
there is a fruit that comes
when our first skirts are soiled
and fallen away.

4

I translate from the dreams of old women.
Drifting through lavender forests,
climbing with ease the yellow mountains
where you can lie down lost in forsythia —

coming to the end of spring
my grandmother kicks off her shoes,
steps out of her faltering body.

The Common

Is wind, the most natural occurrence,
a messenger sent without words or form
filling whatever presents itself?
Now the beech tree's leaves shimmer
like angels on a pin.

An old woman crosses the Common at dawn.
Surely deranged, I think. What tumultuous creatures
does she urge, swooping her arms? What long wails
in no language I ever heard. I see nothing.
Then suddenly all is wings, a great rush of pigeons
as if the gray sky had opened and spilled itself out.

As if all along they'd been there tunneling
through despair like the upward sweep of trees
in bloom when the fog thins, and light
blazing on water spread before me
when I get to the end of myself
and lean at the rail of the last word
trusting what I don't understand.

POETRY FROM ALICE JAMES BOOKS